Limitless

New Poems and Other Writings

By
Danna Faulds

Peaceable Kingdom Books
Greenville, Virginia

Copyright © 2009
Danna Faulds

All rights reserved. No part of this book may be reproduced without written permission from the author.

ISBN 978-0-9744106-6-1

Cover Photograph: Bright Spiral Galaxy M81 in Ultraviolet from Galex. Credit: NASA, JPL-Caltech, Galex Team, J. Huchra et al. (Harvard CfA)

Additional copies of this book, and all poetry books by Danna Faulds
are available by mail.
Send $15.00 (includes postage) to:
Danna Faulds
53 Penny Lane
Greenville VA 24440
The author may be e-mailed at
yogapoems@aol.com

Printed in the U.S.A. by
Morris Publishing
3212 East Highway 30
Kearney NE 68847
1-800-650-7888

For Rumi, Hafiz, Lalla,
Kabir, Emily Dickinson,
Walt Whitman, Mary Oliver,
Paul Weiss, David Whyte,
and all poets whose words
bring the limitless
to life.

Other Poetry Books by Danna Faulds

Go In and In: Poems From the Heart of Yoga (2002)

One Soul: More Poems From the Heart of Yoga (2003)

Prayers to the Infinite: New Yoga Poems (2004)

From Root to Bloom: Yoga Poems and Other Writings (2006)

Danna's poetry also appears in:

Kripalu Yoga: A Guide to Practice On and Off the Mat, by Richard Faulds and the Senior Teachers of Kripalu Center for Yoga and Health (Bantam, 2006)

Sayings of Swami Kripalu: Inspiring Quotes From a Contemporary Yoga Master, edited with introduction and commentary by Richard Faulds.

Swimming with Krishna: Teaching Stories from the Kripalu Yoga Tradition, edited with commentary by Richard Faulds.

The Enlightenment Teachings of Yogeshwar Muni, American Disciple of Swami Kripalu, edited by Richard Faulds.

*****

All books except *Kripalu Yoga: A Guide to Practice On and Off the Mat* are available by e-mailing Danna at yogapoems@aol.com. Wholesale prices are available for purchases of 5 books or more.

Introduction

There was a time not that long ago when I was actively afraid to meditate. Sitting still felt like an invitation to be judged by an all-seeing, all-knowing God-on-high. Growing quiet inside seemed impossible, and if I approached anything like inner silence, I feared falling into nothingness, never to emerge again.

After years of doing yoga, meditation slowly became part of my practice. Now, it is a rare day when I skip meditating. Where my writing was once intimately linked with my yoga practice, it is more common now for a poem to emerge at the end of meditation than in the midst of postures. Hatha yoga continues to be an important touchstone, but it is my time on the cushion that provides most of the fuel for my evolutionary journey.

Sitting for 20 minutes to an hour each morning, I've grown familiar with a variety of meditation techniques. Some days I watch my breath or witness the sensations, thoughts, and feelings moving through me. Other days I sit in the truth of "what is," and let go of the need to change anything at all. One morning may find me journeying back to the root of awareness, before ideas or sense impressions. The next, I'm practicing self-inquiry, asking who it is that witnesses, or what is true in this moment.

There are also mornings when I get caught in an eddy of thought and whirl there for the duration of my meditation. Usually though, whenever I am able to apply one of these techniques with focus, it takes me beneath the choppy surface of the mind and onto one of two paths, described in Sanskrit as neti-neti and asmi-asmi. While I've never been a fan of Sanskrit, these terms encompass ideas that take whole paragraphs to explain in English.

Neti-neti, translates as "not this, not this." The basis of classical yoga, neti-neti is the way of negation. It is a path that reveals who I really am by cutting away all the things I am not. I am not this body or this migraine pain. I am not my thoughts, even when the inner voices grow so loud they drown out everything else. I am not my personal stories or my opinions. I am not the fear that threatens to swallow me, not my wisest and most insightful writing, or even the most profound "aha" to come out of my spiritual practice.

When I am stripped bare of everything else, my experience is that the unchanging, deathless truth of me is transcendent, non-dual awareness. The only problem is that after walking the path of neti-neti for a time, I chafe against saying "no" to everything. At my core, there is a "yes" that must be embodied and expressed, an embrace so wide I ignore it at my peril.

Asmi-asmi is the flip side of neti-neti. Translated as "this too, this too," asmi-asmi is a practice that comes from tantra – the path of immanence. Identifying with the whole, I find spirit, truth, and oneness everywhere I look. I am this aging body on its slow march toward death. I am everything my senses can experience and more. I am this mind and its dramatic machinations. I am the yearnings of the heart, the full spectrum of feelings, and the peace that passes understanding. I am the worst of my poems, and the best. I am the infinite reach of nature, sky, and stars. The only word that matters on this path is "Yes." I include, include, include until the individual "me" blips out, leaving only unity.

My personal preference has always been for sensory experience, embodiment, and inclusion. For that reason, I resisted the practice of neti-neti because it felt dry and life-denying. I wasn't interested in transcendence if it came at the expense of being fully alive in my body and actively engaged in life. Fortunately, I overcame my resistance and discovered that when I really focused on bare awareness, on what was not thought, not sensation, not my personal accumulation of conditioning and beliefs, I landed in a very spacious place of pure potential.

Exploring that potential one morning, it occurred to me that practicing at either end of the spectrum -- neti-neti or asmi-asmi -- might result in the same experience. Inquiring deeper, I asked myself if ultimate negation and absolute inclusion could exist simultaneously. "That's impossible," my rational mind answered. "It's happening," my experience whispered softly in my ear. In that moment, I fell into a profound inner silence – the silence that flashes into existence when opposites unite. Outside of time, I disappeared into the limitless.

Perhaps I can best describe my current practice as "both/and." Instead of focusing only on neti-neti, or giving myself over entirely to the practice of asmi-asmi, I am plumbing the depths of paradox where "no" and "yes" coexist.

Quantum physics speaks of "deep truths" in which two seemingly opposite realities are simultaneously true. Light is both a wave and a particle, a fact that shouldn't be possible, yet it is. Similarly, I shouldn't be able to negate my way back to my true nature and say "yes" to all existence at the same time, but I regularly do so.

I am sharing my experience with the paths of neti-neti and asmi-asmi because many of the poems in this book speak to one end of my practice spectrum or the other. A few describe what it's like when the two poles come together. Here's a recent example:

> Light and Laughing
>
> In the light and laughing space
> where Not-This and All-This
> are both true, the whirl of
> thought dissolves. The mind
> drowns in paradox. Awareness
> neither reaches out, nor reaches in,
> and time hangs suspended.

Sometimes the first line of a poem like this one interrupts me during meditation and insists on being written down – NOW! Other days I sit through my whole meditation session, then write the words "This is what I have to say to you" at the top of the page and see what comes. A few days ago I wrote:

> This is what I have to say to you. Put up
> no resistance to the day as it unfolds.
> Watch the play of opposites, your likes
> and dislikes, thoughts you would draw
> close and those from which you would
> recoil. What if, for this moment, you let
> it all be as it is? What if you interfere
> with nothing?

Become the subject – vast, bare, always aware. Of course there are objects. Do not try to shut them out or change what is. Sense impressions, circumstances, the day's events move forward on the wheel of time while you are timeless, the silent subject of the whole, pure potential, simply there.

When the entire universe blazes into being, take it all inside yourself, without exception. When the only word is "Yes," when your point of view dissolves into every viewpoint and no viewpoint at all, when the Big Bang is happening in every instant, you are fully and finally alive.

Like a faucet that dispenses water from a hidden reservoir below the earth, this kind of writing allows the formless mystery to flow into my conscious life. What I tap into when I write from the quiet of my meditation cushion feels limitless. My ability to attune may be constrained by surface disturbances or conditioned beliefs, but the repository of wisdom, energy, and creativity is infinite.

Each morning finds me at the edge of my current experience, writing about where I am stuck, where I am learning to let go, and what is calling me forward right now. My writing practice is fulfilling, alive, and compelling because it emerges organically from my personal evolution. Words on the page, both poetry and prose, are the record of my struggle, surrender, suffering, ease, joy, silence, and delight. They are the bread crumbs left behind as I move beyond my comfort zone and into the unknown.

While this is mostly a book of poetry, I've chosen to include a number of prose pieces that brought me helpful messages. Using "This is what I have to say to you" as a trigger phrase, I let words flow onto the page without editing and am always surprised by the result. This technique and every writing technique I've ever tried is just a way to access the creative flow that springs from somewhere outside the thinking mind. This one happens to work well for me.

In the end, writing remains a profound mystery. It is an act of intimate listening and receptivity, but I can't pinpoint exactly what it is that I hear. I know that what the Quakers call the "still, small voice" can be easily shouted down by worry, fear, doubt, or inattention. That's where disciplined practice comes in. I also know that the inner voice, whispering the first line of a poem so softly I could easily ignore it, can't be called forth by will. When I try to make it happen, meaningful writing eludes me. It is the choice to surrender, relax, be present, and let go that best serves my writing. When I can let it happen, it's there morning after morning, as reliable as sunrise. Although I never know what will show up, the perfect message always appears.

The moment of unknowing when the pen is poised above the page has become a potent metaphor for me. As I learned to let go in my writing practice, I became more able to release into the reality of life unfolding. These days I struggle less to make my outer circumstances match my desires and expectations. I have grown more comfortable with the unknown. Life flows with greater ease – except when it doesn't.

Over time, writing has introduced me to a better version of myself, one that remained hidden until words and phrases birthed it into the light of day. Writing has not only given me a means of expression, but it has helped evolve the "me" that is expressing. Catalyzing the full spectrum of development, writing helped me heal, grow, and integrate the power of awakening into daily life. Even as I write this, it is still carrying me forward, helping me explore new ground. My gratitude for the mysteries of meditation, yoga, life, and writing knows no bounds.

Danna Spitzform Faulds
March, 2009

Acknowledgements

To my husband, Richard Faulds, I offer my profound appreciation for a life and love deep enough to make the writing of these poems possible. Your editorial skills and creative comments enriched every page. Your being enriches my life.

To readers of my poetry who have shared my words with family, friends, yoga students, and workshop participants, your support means more than you will ever know.

A number of friends regularly reached out with understanding, inspiration, and love, helping to keep me going even when the way wasn't easy or clear. Special thanks to Jessica Atcheson, Tara Brach, Jonathan Foust, Heidi Hackford, Margaret Klapperich, Kathy Kuser, Adele and Justin Morreale, and Grace Welker.

As for my family, I could never do what I do without you. John and Kay Faulds, and the Spitzform clan, Hal, Marianne, and Peter, thank you for your love.

To friends who hosted workshops, poetry readings, Kripalu gatherings, or opened the sanctuary of their homes to me and my husband, my gratitude knows no bounds: Marcy and Bruce Balter, Mary Lou and George Buck, Lisette and Phil Cooper, Martha Harbison, Martha and Terry Maguire, and the Morreales. Many of the poems in this book were written in your homes.

There are a number of people I rarely see but whose presence in my life makes a difference nonetheless: James Baraz, Toni Burbank, Stephen Cope, Amy and Yoganand Michael Carroll, Anne Davidson, Malay Desai, Yogi Amrit Desai, Jack Glasser, Ann Greene, Sneha Karen Jegart, Guy Kettelhack, Sudha Carolyn Lundeen, Vandita Kate Marchesiello, Todd Norian, Lawrence Noyes, Deva Parnell, Len and Ling Poliandro, Marc and Meryl Rudin, Mickey Singer, Steve Smaha, Premshakti Mary Stout, Marc Paul Volavka, and Paul Weiss. Gratitude also to WWPL work colleagues Arthur Link and Connie Murray. To each one of you, my heartfelt thanks for the light you bring to this world.

Limitless

Sun says, "Be your own
illumination." Wren says,
"Sing your heart out,
all day long." Stream says,
"Do not stop for any
obstacle." Oak says,
"When the wind blows,
bend easily, and trust
your roots to hold."
Stars say, "What you see
is one small slice of a
single modest galaxy.
Remember that vastness
cannot be grasped by mind."
Ant says, "Small does not
mean powerless." Silence
says nothing. In the quiet,
everything comes clear.
I say, "Limitless." I say,
    "Yes."

High Dive

I stand on the high board,
toes gripping the edge,
palms sweating. There are
only two choices – dive or
flee, and neither seems
acceptable to me – not the
leap from such a height,
not the feel of cold steel
rungs beneath my feet.
I am frozen in time, not here
or there, not now or then.

Finally, I take a breath,
steady shaky legs,
and launch myself into
emptiness. Gravity claims
me then, and I am flying
down and under, water
rushing past closed eyes
and outstretched hands.
And then I'm gasping
at the surface, looking
up at that distant board,
amazed and unafraid.

Moment of Release

You've held the pose for
so long. All your sweat
and effort, all your focus,
courage, and connection
have brought you to this
moment of release.

Receive it with your
whole being, knowing
that you can't control
where surrender takes you.

You can only give yourself
over to the flow of breath
and consciousness that leads
into the clear light of
your remembering again.

The Soul's Whole Truth

Here, with no audience
but trees, let your heart
speak freely. Where the
elders once gathered to
pass an eagle feather
round their sacred circle,
hand to hand, find your
life's bold path and let
it call you forward.

Take the feather when it
comes to you, and dare
to be transformed.
As wings spread wide,
rise above the tree tops,
open sky inviting you into
the soul's whole truth.

Grace

All sounds
spring from
silence.

All things,
seen and unseen,
come from
truth.

Knowing this
to be the case,
why not surrender
fully to the
flow of grace?

True Right Now

Truth is true
right now; all-
pervading, creative,
infinite, and free.
I can easily
evade it,
but this is no
practice life.
This is the real
deal, slipping
through my hands
like sand.

Truth is true
right now, but
only if I lose
myself in it,
only if I'm
willing to be
used by it,
to trade in my
illusions and open
to what's real.

Stream Music

Stream plays its
downhill music
with such fluency
that I stop my
walk to listen
on the bridge.

Water races over
rocks, melody
changing with
each moment.

Nature weaves
itself into my
awareness until
I too am humming,
my voice and a
nearby crow's
mingling so easily
there seem to be
no fixed boundaries
here in the woods,
thrumming with
the earth's slow
heartbeat.

Trail of Bread Crumbs

Poetry is the sound
a soul makes as it
comes to know the
whole. It's the trail
of bread crumbs left
behind as a seeker
climbs to find the
clearest vista.

A poem is the
universe speaking
in a unique voice
about anything that
strikes its fancy.
It's a moment fully
lived and crystallized
in words that strip
the wrapping
from the gift.

The Universal Church of Silent Grace

No roof but sky and stars,
no walls at all, no pews
or carpet, The Universal
Church of Silent Grace is
every place and no place.

Birds provide the music,
and the sun, that shiny
chandelier, gives ample
light 'til nightfall.

The service doesn't start
nor does it end, and when
it rains, God's blessings
fall equally upon those
who raise their eyes in
appreciation, and those
who, like the robins,
stare only at the earth,
patiently waiting for
the miracle of worms.

Like a Lover

I never noticed,
before this,
how each moment
parts its lips
to kiss me with
the passion of a
lover, lost in bliss.

This is what I have to say to you. Receive the interconnected majesty of All That Is. When a cardinal sings in your yard, something very like a cat picks up its ears a hundred light years from here. When you feel grateful for your life, across the world, someone's heart lifts for no apparent reason. The universe is like that, invisible threads connecting the granite bones of mountains with black holes, earthworms joined with sound waves, coke cans inextricably linked to crocuses. Some call this Indra's net. Some say the world is One. I say that language may be limited, but oneness is unthinkably inclusive.

Nothing you do or say, imagine or pray is outside creation's web. Know yourself as vastness and someone you never met may find themselves directly experiencing truth for the first time. The universe is like that, light pouring into light, love increasing, the awareness of connection growing wider and wider until inside is outside, outside is inside, and all we're left with is miracles.

Open

Nothing to wall out
or hold in.
Open like the
wide sky at twilight.
Open as the ocean
or the reach of
the unknown.
Open as a heart
that chooses
not to close.

Gift from the Mystery

When I listen, words are everywhere,
riding the air currents like broad-winged hawks.
Poems are born in the molten centers
of stars. Exploding into supernovas,
they travel light years to reach this spinning
ball of water and dirt, then wait eons more
to tell their tale.

When I'm lucky, a whole poem
arrives at once, sliding out of my psyche
as if it was mine, unexpectedly illuminating
this corner of the universe.

Words are everywhere when I grow still.
Whispered by lovers in mid-kiss
or sung as a lullaby; shouted in rage or prayed
by a saint whose face is lit with inner flames,
it's all fuel for my fire, grist for the turning
wheel of transformation, a gift from the
mystery to this finite world of form.

Nothing More Is Needed

Inside the hot, hard knot
of raw sensation, here inside
the heart of fear and pain,
I find the flame of truth.

My path is through –
diving right into whatever
past conditioning bids
me hide or push aside.

When I soften, open, accept,
and receive, the flow of
energy is immediate.
Nothing more is needed
to awaken completely
than the intimate
experience of now.

Daffodils

A hundred daffodils
lift their faces
to the sun,
never noticing
their own golden light.

Bare Awareness

Bare awareness
awake to its
true nature –
limitless and
vast, nothing to
grasp, no masks
or name tag.

What am I beyond
the answers of the
mind, outside
anything I can
find by seeking?

What is true
right now, and
what is transitory?

The witness watches
thoughts spin their
convincing stories
out of thin air and
doesn't care how
often I forget
that freedom is
the truth of being,
and no part of truth
is ever separate
from what is.

Let the Mind Be the Mind

Let the mind be the mind.
Behind its restless activity,
just one layer deeper
is stillness, and beneath
even that, is an ocean
of mystery and truth.

Swim in this eternal sea
until you know yourself
to be infinity, and bring
that knowing back into
your day. Why struggle
to be what you are already?

Let the mind be the mind,
but don't bind yourself
to its limited reality.
Trust your experience of
vastness. Trust the truth
that never loses potency
or disappears in fear.

Let the mind be the mind
and identify not with
thought, but silence.

Love Puddle

Do not bloody your fingers
trying to untie the knot.
The rope is thick and
rough, your fingers slim
and delicate. Instead of
struggling, turn to face
the moon. Let love pour
out of you and mingle
with her silver light.

Jump into that love puddle,
splashing until you laugh,
dancing until your bare feet
leave moon tracks on the grass.
With the night sky as your
witness, you'll find the knot
undone, the rope coiled and
hung, the moon winking one
conspiratorial eye and
smiling at your surprise.

Change

Change proclaims its
dominance. "Just try
and stay the same,"
it taunts. "See how
long the status quo
will last before it's
blasted into newness
by the now."

Change isn't always
flashy like the Grand
Canyon. Sometimes
it's subtle, like the
blinking of an eyelash
or the floating of a
feather on the wind.

Say yes, and change
will take you somewhere
unexpected. Say no,
and you'll end up in
the same place,
resisting all the while.

I'd rather go willingly
and see if the journey
itself just might be
worth the ride.

The Dove

A lovely bird the
color of pearls, the
dove found nothing
on her first journey
off the ark but restless
waves that stretched
in all directions.

On her second try,
the dove discovered
an olive tree, and
rested in its branches
as the water danced
beneath her. Plucking
a leaf, she carried it
in her beak back to the
bleating sheep and
chattering monkeys,
back to Noah and
his family.

Certain that life
was never meant
to be spent inside a
wooden cage, when
the day for her third
flight arrived,
the dove flew off.
Straining his eyes,
Noah could just
make her out, a speck
on the horizon,
untethered now, and
climbing higher.

This is what I have to say to you. Use your discontent, your longing, the sense that you are bereft of connection, use everything around you to nudge you into choosing joy. Make the choice not because life is as you wish, but because life is as it is. Resist and you know suffering. Jump in with both eyes open and you can drown in bliss.

It doesn't seem possible, I know. You feel broken, disconnected, less than whole. Ask if awareness shares your restlessness. Ask if the infinite cares that your emotional state is tenuous at best. Ask if your dreary thoughts should be believed and if anything real stands between you and All That Is. Use the answers you receive to open a crack in the wall of separation. Find a door and stick your foot in so it can't close even if your doubts grow huge.

"I can't get there from here," you say. My reply is that there is nowhere to go. You are already home. Embrace your immortal soul, the flame that cannot be doused by wind or rain. Embrace the truth of you today.

Burn the Rope

Burn the rope of
past conditioning,
or slice right
through, awareness
like a blade that
cannot be stopped
by any obstacle.

Without the history
of who you've
been, what is the
essence of your
soul's expression?

When you allow
the moment to
offer up its perfect
response, what is
the free and true
experience of you?

Ten Thousand Things

The Big Bang is
still happening.
From nothing springs
ten thousand things –
starlings and eagles,
mitochondria and
mountain breezes,
gallows and galaxies.

When I am open,
uninterrupted creativity
flows through me,
shaping life at the
speed of light
or inviting me to
rest in silence.

Forgiveness

Take all your sins and
shortcomings, every last
mountain and molehill
of your past, and give
them over to the waves.

"That's too easy," you say,
but I tell you there is light
hidden beneath your fear
and a free spirit waiting
to soar with the sea gulls
the moment you relinquish
your tight grip on
guilt or innocence.

Receive the blessings of
the salty spray, the
benediction of the cormorant.
Forgiveness looks like
the delight in your eyes
as you wave goodbye
to the shoreline.

Neither Cruel Nor Kind

Cat leaps.
Bird shrieks.
Single feather
flutters to
the grass.

The day,
neither cruel
nor kind,
continues
on its way
without a
backward
glance.

Turning Inward

At the moment of
turning inward, time
loses its grip. There is
only the press of palm
against palm, the reach
and stretch of limbs,
the sound of breath
slipping out and in
to deliver its gift.

Energy follows focus,
body bowing low, arms
and fingers tingling.
When I let awareness
and sensation lead,
mystery enfolds me.

Circumference

I used to see a dichotomy,
a careful circle drawn and
labeled, "This is the divine."

Over time, the outline disappeared.
Now human and divine
share the same expanse, all of life
infused with just one truth.

Even at my most confused,
when I've proven just how
clueless and forgetful I can be,
even then I am not lost or separate
because the circumference of the
circle is immeasurable.

Outside the Box

Maybe there's no box
to think outside.
Maybe there's no lock,
no door, or key.
Perhaps there's just the
scared, small me
holding tight to turf
that isn't mine,
trying to be somebody.

I struggle for release.
I seek and strive,
all the while failing to see
the obvious.
The only walls in front
of me are those
I've built myself,
the fortress of my personality
so well defended it seems
impenetrable.

What I create,
I can take down – or maybe
I am free right now.

Gardener's Creed

I believe in the creative
energy of sun and soil,
rain, and spring days
giving way to heat.
I believe in seeds, those
miraculous containers
of rebirth, a whole
garden sprouting
into being from a few
paper packets neatly
stamped with planting
dates. I believe in the
healing power of sowing,
weeding, and harvesting,
the complex tangle of
my day giving way to the
immediacy of ripe snow
peas hiding beneath
their sheltering leaves –
waiting to be found.

The Door Is Always Open

Fear. Pain.
Dark moods.
Despairing moments.
Plentiful distractions.

The human drama
plays through me
as it always has,
with one abiding
difference.

Knowing what
I am opens a door
to truth. Sometimes
I step across that
threshold and
sometimes I don't,
but the door
is always open.

River of Light

A shimmering river of light
reaches from the moon
to me. The opaque surface
of the bay changes with the
mood of sky, here a sparkle
of stars, there a wisp of
shadow. Waves breathe
and break, a living
invitation to let go.

In this alchemy of wind
and tide, the time feels
right to consummate my
long affair with the Beloved.
Do I dare? The night breeze
lifts the hair from my neck
and I know I can't withhold
even the smallest or most
hidden part of me as I dissolve
inside the ocean's soul.

This is what I have to say to you. Don't feel it. Don't think it. Don't ponder if it's true. Be the Great Awareness having this moment of human experience. Be the energy of the universe animating this vehicle of bone and flesh and nerve impulses. Be the wordless certainty of infinite amazement.

You can't do this in half-measures, with doubt dripping from you like rain drops from moist leaves. Be the awakening so completely that it soaks you through, digests you, uses every morsel and cell, leaving nothing to feel confusion, doubt, or fear. Express the least or most of which you are capable and still you are the Great Awareness burning bright, setting fire to the night of your imagined unworthiness.

Mud of the Moment

Truth lives in the mud
of this moment. It exists
in the messy interplay of
emotions and relationship,
in the personality traits
I'd rather leave behind.

To experience truth
doesn't take sainthood,
or dissolving my desires.
It requires diving into
the muck and mire of
what's here, feeling
the anxiety or fear,
knowing the entirety
of me without hiding
from the shadows or
from light.

Choosing to be whole,
awareness makes the
leap to see that I am
truth – always was,
and always will be –
the radiant singularity,
the infinite in human
form. The lotus never
blooms without
sinking roots in mud.

The Pendulum Swings

Have patience. The pendulum
that swung too far in one
direction will swing back.
At the moment of its turning,
everything hangs in the balance.
All the momentum of past actions
is suspended in mid-air, and
those who care about what
happens next are poised with it.

There is a long and anxious
pause before the motion shifts,
and then a sense of free fall,
when the world is turned on
its head and nothing is known
or normal. Have patience then,
and do not rush to either extreme.
The way will paint its own arrows
on the trees if you can wait for clarity.

Before the Beginning

Mystery infuses
every phase
of growth –
the first green
shoot to push
its way above
the dirt, leaves
and buds, blossoms,
fruit, and seeds,
even the dried
stalks that rattle
in the cold season –
each stage is
equally honorable.
What was present
before the beginning
will be there
after the end.

Call and Response

In this call and response
of love, waves and bird
songs speak to my true
nature. Ocean and osprey,
mockingbird and me all
share a common tongue.

Essence touches essence,
soul connects with soul.
It isn't the differences
I see, but unity,
Spirit bestowing countless
names on wonder.

Pray and Wait

Find the way back to
your heart's own altar.
If God seems absent,
pray and wait. If you
feel forsaken, grow so
still inside that you
can hear the whisper,
"I am with you."

Something is alive in
your tears of longing,
awake in the very
places that feel empty
and bereft of light.
Pray, and the day is
different, the sweet
taste of the divine
like water turned
suddenly to wine.

Why I'm Here

Hello day, I say.
I'm here to be your
co-conspirator.
I'm here to grow
less respectful of
my limits with each
hour until the idea
of limits disappears
altogether. I'm here
to write an anthem
to the sky and sing
it aloud, even if I
can't yet reach
the high notes.

Soul Self

Who feels this sense of
trepidation, this unsettled
anxiety clinging like wet
sheets? It isn't the soul
self, radiating energy and
light. It isn't the whole
self, alive, creative, wise.
I locate my anxiety inside
the fear that something
should be different here.

The small me generates
expectations and paints
masks to hide behind,
while the great self
points to the absolute
perfection of the universe
and says, "You are that,"
says, "Don't for a moment
confuse the body-mind
with what you really are."

Joyful Noise

Pick up the trumpet
and put it to your lips.
Who cares that you
don't know how to
blow or where to
place your fingers?
Your joyful noise
will make a difference
in this world.

Are you so sure you
know what music is
that you would resist
the impulse, silence
the notes that rise
from who knows where?
Far better to risk failure
than never hear the
melody that's been
waiting for a lifetime
to be shared.

Source of Peace

Turning inward
to the source of
peace, I take refuge
in the easy sigh
of breath released.

Awareness spirals
behind the mind,
finding quiet,
a temporary respite
from the storm of
thought.

I arrived here by
the simplest route,
using movement
to grow still,
choosing to follow
breath into silence.

The tension I held
onto like a shield
disappeared when
I finally allowed
myself to feel.

Beneath the Beating Wings

A swooping hawk scooped
a sparrow off the deck before
my eyes could register the
scene. A feathered blur,
a squawk of fright, and strong
talons bore the struggling
prize away. I was oddly
shaken, as if it was my life
taken in that instant,
my full and precious life
disappearing in a flash
beneath the beating wings.

This is what I have to say to you. Open to the living lineage of light. Visible or invisible, the truth is alive right now, and you can embody what you are by aligning with that power.

Open to the grace of all the ages flowing through you like a raging river or an underground stream trickling into caves and dark places. Your initiation awaits you in a dream or in the flesh. Do not doubt your experience, but go forth in glory to serve the timeless and the time-bound with equal parts enthusiasm, wisdom, and strength.

Release

I lay myself down
on the welcoming
ground, the earth's
spine becoming mine.
Peace seeps into
heavy limbs and
slows my heartbeat
to the pace of
nature. I take refuge
in the quiet, and let
my burdens go,
one by one, until
the earth and I
both float in the
same vast and
holy silence.

Peter's Plea

Peter held his head
with calloused hands.
"The Master said I
would be his rock,
but instead, three
times I denied him.
Three times I chose
life over truth and
fear over love.
The Master said
"Blessed are the
pure of heart,"
but my impurity
hangs upon me like
low clouds upon the
Sea of Galilee.

I thought to follow
Judas to the tree,
but then I could not
make amends or
bear witness to the
miracles I've seen.

In my misery I cried
out in the night,
"Forgive me Lord.
I do not deserve your
pardon, but without
forgiveness, I cannot
live." It was so still
I could hear fish

pulling up the weeds
and chewing with
their tiny teeth. Not
even the wind blew.

I heard nothing in
reply and thought
for sure my plea had
been denied, but that
night I had a dream.

The Master placed
his hands upon my
head and said,
"Forgive yourself as
I forgive all who turn
to me and ask. Let past
shadows fall away and
make of your life an
offering, with all your
yearning turned to good.
Choose to do your humble
work and leave the fruits
to me. Speak truthfully
of what you've seen and
of the inner changes
wrought by time and life
and the spirit of the Most
High. Find me inside
every act and prayer,
in every pair of feet that
walks the path or stumbles
and gets up again to journey
further. I am alive inside
you, now and always."

Peter raised his eyes and
looked into his open palms.
Big as bowls, his hands
were, and he gazed at the
scars and lines, the etchings
of his simple life.

"It was just a dream, you
see," he said, "and yet it
was more than that to me.
It was the Master's blessing
clear as if he'd said it to
my face. And I'm telling
you that dragging your past
around forever doesn't make
sense. If I can start fresh,
anyone can," Peter said
as he reached down to
retrieve his net.

The Whole Array

This life isn't about
slicing off the parts
I don't like to be
left with those I do.
I choose the whole
array – night and day,
ease and its opposite,
the squeaky wheel
and the grease gun.

Push any piece of
life away, and a key
that could have
opened a door is
lost, tossed out with
the trash. I pray for
the courage to receive
the full catastrophe,
however it appears
to me, without
needing to push back.

How I Feel Right Now

I've misplaced my optimistic nature, or perhaps it crawled away while I was looking in the opposite direction.

In any case, my inner world is uniformly gray, and I'm imprisoned by the fear that life will always be this way. No amount of wishful thinking shifts my mood.

I feel disconnected, doomed to hear the chorus of self-doubts, the harsh inner voices whispering their pessimistic predictions and gloomy assessments of my worth.

My only goal is to draw no conclusions, choosing not to make the moment mean anything except that this is how I feel right now.

Your Full Expression

Stretch long, and longer still. Reach wide until the expanding space inside is filled with light. What began as willful practice now generates its own energy.

Offer this, the radiance of you, back to the universe. The give and take of breath calls forth your full expression, birthing something new, something crucial, that no posture can contain.

Tickled

This moment is a rosebud, and I am at the center of the bloom. Petals open one by one until I am in full sun, tickled by the tongues of butterflies.

Except When I Forget

I've fallen in love
with my own life
in all its gloriously
messy imperfection.

I hold the moment
close, saying "yes"
with each breath,
saying "thank you,"
except when I forget.

The forgetting is
complete, like amnesia
or the densest fog that
grips me until it lifts
and I remember how
simple it is to give
myself completely to
the miracle of what is.

Bold Strength

The clematis vine
outgrew its trellis
long ago. It twines
around the gladiola
leaves and peonies
seeking something
tall to climb.

I, too, outgrew the
place where I was
planted and sought
a structure to bear
me up until
I found my own
bold strength.

This is what I have to say to you. Live from the limitless. Give up the small sense of "I" that longs for control and yearns to do things right. The surrender required is to let the whole come through you instead of the part. Admit the defeat of the unique, the boundaried being trying desperately to be special. Surrender that false identity in favor of your true self, the timeless being that emerges from emptiness, dissolves back into the infinite, and listens to the creative overflow of silence. Allow the limitless to be your guide, your shape, your light, and the truth you choose to steer by.

Come Forth

Come forth, awakened one.
Come forth like a deer
breaking out of deep
woods into a clearing.
The sum of your time
here is measured not
by what you've kept
hidden, but by acts
that shine like sapphires,
kindnesses you've freed
from the cage of your
fears, truths you've
let loose into the world
like bolts of lightning
on a moonless night.

Magic Carpet

I do not know
how to align my
spine with truth,
or stretch far
enough to touch
the stars. How to
really let go is
still a mystery
to me. I can't
seem to tie my
life up neatly
in a perfect bow,
but when I let
the ribbon blow
freely in the
wind, it weaves
a magic carpet
I could never
have foreseen.

Without Apology

Seeking just begets
more seeking, an
endless quest to
fill the void.
When I sit with
the soul's silence,
seeking yields to
finding. Only then
can I choose to
know what I know
and be what I
really am, openly,
and without apology.

Lunacy or Liberation

On spirals of mist I rise
up and up, until the houses
below look like push pins
on a topographic map.

A passing goose salutes
me with one wing, and I
remember I can't fly,
but it's too late now
for doubt. Up and up,
my breath like a jet trail,
humming a tune of my
own creation.

Whoever would believe
that wings could be my
destiny, neither angel nor
eagle, but something quite
distinct, the product of my
own sweet dream of freedom
and my wildest imaginings.

I am up above even the hint
of humdrum or ordinary,
where every beat of wing
is miraculous and I'm singing
aloud: "Who knew this was
possible? Who knew how
the perfect curve of earth
could disappear in stars?"

Yoga's Gift

Merge movement with
unchanging stillness.
Blend stretch with breath
and depth-mind awareness.
Bridging the inner and
outer realms is yoga's gift,
allowing layer after layer
to peel away until the truth
is indisputable, and I am
left suspended like
a drop of dew, poised
and lucid in the quiet.

Silent Celebration

A catbird tries to fly
against the wind only
to be blown backward.
I know that feeling –
setting out with certainty
and arriving somewhere
entirely different. When
I respond with acceptance
to my unexpected
destination, the sun
clangs its cymbals of
light in silent celebration.

Point of Radiance

Find the point of radiance
in your heart. Whether
that be passion, pleasure,
or pain so deep it's etched
in blood, follow where
your true heart leads.

When it seems there is no
light, look carefully,
for it is always there,
that ember of the God-force.

It may be hidden in a dim
corner or buried beneath
a pile of regrets, but it's
there nonetheless, that
spark of divine essence,
illuminating your next step.

Imagine

Imagine a patchwork quilt without a seam. Imagine a stream without a point of origin, or sunlight without the contrast of a shadow.

In your mind's eye, see an unimpeded flow of energy arising from a single source, expressing itself in countless forms, each imbued with the selfsame spark of truth.

This is what you really are.

Just Be

Finally, I am slowing down.
After weeks of doing, I have
a moment to just be.
Serenity must be chosen,
the wave of relaxation washing
through me not by chance,
but choice. I consciously
give myself over to the tide
of peace that easily receives
the burdens I release.

A New Address

The answer isn't austerity.
It isn't fundamentalism
or hedonistic abandon.

The answer isn't a battle
to the death with the small self,
nor is it feeding every
ego need and preference.

Trying to beat my mind
into submission just
leaves me weary and defeated.
How then shall I live?

The answer is to give myself
into the unknown until letting go
is second nature,
until the enormity
occurs to me as home.

This is what I have to say to you. Throw off the bonds of your conditioning and fear and celebrate the wonder of being here. Experience this moment as it is, connected by breath and essence to the whole. You couldn't be separate if you tried.

Live this day as if the earth exhales blessings in your direction, as if trees speak their deepest secrets in your ear, as if bird songs can lift you outside your ordinary state of mind and bring you into truth.

Be the creative juice flowing through the universe. Be compassion in action and wholeness in motion. Be silence and stillness, the ocean of love so palpable that not one cell of you disputes the truth that you are that. Be so open to your destiny that it unfurls like a banner in the sky, a sign saying "Live until you die with gratitude, generosity, and grace."

The Only Breath That Counts

If I'm waiting for
safety, there's no hope.
If I'm waiting for the
perfect day, the moment
when outer circumstance
and inner mood line up
like sunlight through
Stonehenge on the
solstice, I might as well
give up. If it's never the
right time to change,
why not be changed now?
Why not say, "This is it.
I'm living as if there's no
tomorrow?" Happy for
no reason, joyful just
because, mindfully taking
the only breath that counts.

Weston Prayer

I pray to stay open today. Open to the unrestrained energy of now. Open to mystery and power. Open to whatever comes. Open to routine and surprises. Open to moving past my first reactions. Open to my imperfections and the divine spark that underlies them. Open to wonder and the everyday grace of life unfolding as it does. Open to events and circumstances that I like, and those I don't. Open to fatigue and overflowing energy. Open to listen and to speak. Open to love in all the ways it manifests. Open to give and to receive. Open to seasons changing, priorities rearranging, nothing staying the same for very long. Open to letting beliefs dissolve into the ether. Open to the direct experience of truth. Open to forgetting and remembering. Open to life and open to death. Open to seeing old patterns and letting them go. Open to fear and courage, ease and difficulty. I pray to stay open.

Queen of My Heart

I sit upon the throne
of life, queen of my
heart, monarch of the
mysteries within me.

I offer praise and
hallelujahs to the day
as it breaks open,
the golden yolk of
sun sharing its
sustenance equally
with seen and unseen.

Tossing my crown
of roses to the sky,
I dance down the
aisle of pine trees,
robed in light, joy
overflowing as I
enter the abode
of my Beloved.

Presence

Always aware,
always there.
Bare, vast,
radiant and free –
the truth of me.

No Corner Is Untouched

The broad, blue bowl of sky
pours light into my eyes
as if there is no end to its
bright treasure. I receive
the sun's gift gratefully,
warmed and glowing to my
bones, all the way down to
the darkest and most hidden
corners that feared they
would always be forgotten.

Loose Ends

Do I focus on loose ends
or on the golden thread
connecting everything
to the present tense?
The thread of openness,
gratitude, and truth wends
its way through every
event and crevice of
consciousness. All the
loose ends are real in
a relative sense, but if
I wait for resolution,
I'll be waiting past my
last breath, asking how
this wondrous life
slipped so quickly
through my fingers.

Wind-Swept World

Flap, flap, glide.
Turkey vultures
ride the rising
currents of air
up and up until
their wing tips are
barely visible,
and this earth
is just a small
distraction in
their silent, wind-
swept world.

Inquiry

Feed the inner fire
with breath, with
inquiry, and the
willingness to see
reality. When the
flames consume the
edges of your life,
invite them into
the center, the core
of your identity,
the innermost chamber
where your deepest
fears reside. Watch
the fire rise, sparks
flying, flames lighting
the open space that
remains when all
else is burned away.

Rememberings

Doubts are endless. I vow
to see through each one
and name the fear beneath.

Fear is bottomless. I vow
to feel it without
believing it is real.

Distractions surround me.
I vow to pay close attention
to what is true.

Escape beckons. I vow to
stay present through the
thousand urges to flee,
the thousand forgettings,
the thousand and one
rememberings.

The Path to Freedom

What is the path to freedom here?
The answer is clear the moment
that I ask. At every fork in the road,
there is a conditioned response
and one that is unpatterned, bold,
and free. The old, known way is
more comfortable, but the other
path holds mystery and wonder.

This is what I have to say to you. Make this day your own. Without having to change even the smallest detail of your outer experience, let your inner world be one of ease, expansion, laughter, and acceptance of what is. Flaws and foibles, failures and doubts are part and parcel of the whole. Instead of looking at them as obstacles, move through them as doorways. Push back, and it's as if a dark cloud covers the face of the sun. Experience them fully, take them in stride, and the day feels magical.

Decide to dance with difficulties, turn challenges into choices, and the way opens before you like the yellow brick road did for Dorothy in Oz. In truth there is no place like home – the home of serenity and strength, the home of self-acceptance and compassion, the home where you can laugh at your mistakes and celebrate being awake.

Whatever Doesn't Serve

What weight can you
put down right now,
willingly relinquishing
the pointed quills of
guilt or judgment?

What burden of the heart
can lift, what dark corner
can be lit, the candle
flickering at first, then
burning bright?

With the next breath,
let it go, that old story
you've told yourself
a million times.

Whatever doesn't serve
you on this path of truth,
leave it behind. Offer
this one gift: the simple
sacrifice that in the giving
sets you free to fully live.

From the Many

(With thanks to Vandita)

My eyes are drawn
by yellow leaves,
bright against a
leaden sky. At first
I think this explosion
of gold is all one tree,
but then I see at least
three trunks. Isn't it
astonishing how
multiplicity gives rise
to unity – that from the
many comes the one?

The Possibility

Do you feel the possibility?
Awakened energy is poised
to flow. Freedom beckons
from every direction.
This is a moment to throw
caution to the wind and dive
right in or fly high above the
rocky terrain of doubt and fear.
You've lived your life
anticipating this opportunity.
Rejoice, for it is here.

No Limit

My overflowing
heart could fill
every chalice,
bowl, and basin
to the brim and
still not be diminished.
There simply is no
limit on love.

And I Must Close My Eyes

Putting aside my mind's agenda,
I melt into the sunrise. Light leaps
outside the silver lining of the
cloud bank in the east and races
to the maples. Clad in the last
remnants of their autumn finery,
the trees receive the sun. Lover and
Beloved meet, and I must close my
eyes to keep from being blinded.

The Lineage Lives

We are the energy of Shiva,
the vastness of the real,
the open space of silence
beyond mind. We are
timeless truth creating
itself anew.

The lineage lives in each
of us who choose to embody
its universal themes and
give shape and texture
to its dreams.

Consort of the Cosmos

Consort of the cosmos,
do not falter at the brink.
Haven't you sought this
transformation all your days?
You will emerge from
the great lovemaking as
a new being. Serve the
whole not by growing
timid, but by throwing
inhibition to the wind.
Union begins with two,
then disappears in one.
If this be death, say yes
until the syllable
reverberates clear through,
until it resounds with such
exuberance that truth is
revealed as nothing more
nor less than you.

Emptiness

The emptiness of which
I speak is not a nihilistic
sump pump of nothing.
This is vastness on the
grandest scale, an open
space of infinitely
connected energy.

Changeless yet flowing,
free and unperturbed
by surface disturbances,
this emptiness is full
of truth. It swallows
the ego, but this is no
black hole.

Instead, it radiates a
pure and steady light,
accessible and endless,
erasing distance,
erasing separation.

The Indescribable

Ever the optimist, I insist
on having my notebook
with me as I sit.

I never know when
inspiration might hit,
when that miniscule
grit of an idea will
get under my skin and
irritate until the pearl
is spit out on the page.

I never know when
the Muse will choose
to speak of being all
things and nothing in
the very same phrase.

I can't tell in advance
if my pen will pause
in the paradox, then
begin again the insane
attempt to describe
the indescribable.

This is what I have to say to you. Every creative act involves taking a journey back to the seed being, back to the truth of your direct experience. Bring consciousness to the dark and silence, to the unconditioned pure potential at your core, and the whole universe comes alive. Energy flows back and forth from formless to form, and relative to absolute. From this energy comes music, painting, movement, poetry, wonder, wisdom, and love.

The creative journey bids you take a leap beyond the known to receive what has been growing outside the reach of your awareness since the Big Bang brought the cosmos into being. You cannot embrace true creativity without being changed in some way from the inside out, nudged toward transformation, revealed to yourself as the light of truth. You cannot give yourself over to the whole without being released from the tyranny of mind or the belief that you are just this finite body.

Receive the miraculous outpouring of life as it is in this moment, in all its perfect imperfection. Receive the truth of you embraced by life and never, ever separate from the Absolute.

Spark to Flame

May the peace of your being
leap from heart to heart
and mind to mind like a
wildfire in dry grass.
Through the simple act of
being present here and now,
may the peace that passes all
understanding be fanned
from spark to flame to
true illumination.

I Have to Laugh

The path to truth is
so wide and universal
that I have to laugh
at my belief that there
could be one way,
one gate, one right
answer, that I could
need to do anything
at all to be complete.

All of Me

I call upon all of me to come forth,
the wild mystery, the nameless one
whose strength and serenity never
ceases to surprise me. I call upon
the vast Self without form or face
to take her place within this skin
and far beyond it.

I open my arms to her, the priestess
kindling the sacred fire in my heart,
the quiet one who wields the pen,
the lover of God and the goddess
who takes the night sky as her bed.

I call upon the truth of me, whole
and unedited, the one who excels
in slow growth and evolutionary
leaps, yogini and poet, receiver of
all that is known and unknown.

I call upon my inner nature
to show herself, be herself,
and breathe with me
the sweet, intoxicating
air of freedom.

Eddies and Currents

Eddies, currents, tides –
life doesn't hide its
thoroughfares, and they
all lead back to the
same wide sea.

Plans and schemes
won't get me there
any more rapidly
then being carried
by the stream.

In truth, it's letting
go and giving up
control that delivers
me into the ocean's
close embrace.

Following a Star

My friends all mocked me
when I set out, led onward
by a star, but I knew it was
my destiny to witness the
birth of something new.

I still don't know my
destination, but I'm drawn
forward day after day and
long into the nights,
traveling by moonlight.

Others say I'm mad,
but I've never felt such
a clear sense of purpose.
I wouldn't give up now,
no matter what was offered.

Following a star – the
whole idea is preposterous,
but here I am, every
fiber of my being awake
to possibility. Maybe I'll
arrive today, or perhaps
tomorrow.

Maybe I'll never arrive,
but at least I will have tried.
Even if all I find beneath
the star is my own face
looking up in wonder,
isn't that enough?

No Mistake

Holding my tension close
is exhausting. I don't
know why I do it –
habit I guess – but when
I let it go, the sense of
relaxation and release
is immediate. My whole
body sighs as ease and
healing bathe each cell
in light. Once the truth
of me has space and
energy to shine forth,
it's clear that the alchemy
of humanity and divinity
is no mistake.

The Luminous Now

Fresh and unexpected,
the scroll of this
moment unrolls slowly,
line by line. There is
no way to look ahead,
or read the ending
first. The luminous
now is never done
with its surprises.

Lake Voice

The frozen lake makes
a sound of its own
creation. Neither creak
nor groan, but a low note
that skates upon the
frigid air and echoes
off the hills.

The lake voice speaks
of cold and mystery,
of water shifting states
from liquid to solid,
molecules expanding
until something gives
and sends a shiver up
the earth's long spine.

Blank Page

On the blank page
of this day, I write
"Yes." I write
"Acceptance."

It's a journey I
take every morning,
the choice to greet
what's here with as
much equanimity
as I can muster.

When my heart
closes in fear or
overwhelm, I pray
"Help me please,"
and a response
always comes.

Courage, strength
or laughter takes
the place of my
despair. I write
"Grateful," and
move on.

Always Into Love

On this voyage of
the soul, may we be
bridge builders,
our common ground
visible beneath the
surface differences.

May we braid the
threads of reconciliation
into a chain of possibility
that joins, heals, and
includes what once
seemed separate.

May our shared prayer
be answered: to grow
so open that there is
no "them" or "us,"
only the One, moving
always into love.

This is what I have to say to you. Go further than your mind can reach, further than your words can speak. Go further than you know, outside of your control. Break your conditioning by letting go and letting go and letting go. Like a twig plucked from a tree, carried a great distance, and woven into a crow's nest, you have no idea of your real destiny.

Keep going until there is nothing left, and you are empty and bereft. Hold that open space. Inhabit the place of not knowing until grace tugs on your awareness and says "Follow me into the center of chaos and serenity. Follow me to what you've always been and always will be."

The truth of you is far beyond what you imagine, simultaneously deathless and here to be lived, then surrendered back into the infinite.

Index of Titles and First Lines

All of Me, 105
All sounds spring from silence, 21
Always aware, always there, 85
Always Into Love, 112
And I Must Close My Eyes, 97
The answer isn't austerity, 80
At the moment of turning inward, 42
Bare Awareness, 32
Bare awareness awake to its true nature, 32
Be the Great Awareness having this moment, 48
Before the Beginning, 51
Beneath the Beating Wings, 58
The Big Bang is still happening, 39
Blank Page, 111
Bold Strength, 69
Broad, blue bowl of sky pours light, 86
Burn the Rope, 38
Call and Response, 52
Cat leaps. Bird shrieks, 41
Catbird tries to fly against the wind, 76
Change, 35
Change proclaims its dominance, 35
Circumference, 43
Clematis vine outgrew its trellis long ago, 69
Come Forth, 71
Come forth, awakened one, 71
Consort of the Cosmos, 99
Daffodils, 31
Do I focus on loose ends or on the golden, 87
Do not bloody your fingers trying to untie, 34
Do you feel the possibility? Awakened energy, 95
The Door Is Always Open, 46
Doubts are endless. I vow to see through, 90
Dove, 36

Eddies and Currents, 106
Emptiness, 100
Ever the optimist, I insist on, 101
Every creative act involves taking a journey, 102
Except When I Forget, 68
Fear. Pain. Dark moods. Despairing Moments, 46
Feed the inner fire with breath, 89
Finally, I am slowing down, 79
Find the point of radiance in your heart, 77
Find the way back to your heart's own altar, 53
Flap, flap, glide. Turkey vultures ride, 88
Following a Star, 107
Forgiveness, 40
Fresh and unexpected, 109
From the Many, 94
Frozen lake makes a sound, 110
Gardener's Creed, 45
Gift from the Mystery, 29
Go further than your mind can reach, 113
Grace, 21
Have patience. The pendulum that swung, 50
Hello day, I say, 54
Here, with no audience but trees, 20
High Dive, 18
Holding my tension close is exhausting, 108
How I Feel Right Now, 65
Hundred daffodils lift their faces to the sun, 31
I believe in the creative energy of sun and soil, 45
I call upon all of me to come forth, 105
I do not know how to align my spine with truth, 72
I Have to Laugh, 104
I lay myself down on the welcoming ground, 60
I Must Close My Eyes, 97
I never noticed, before this, 26
I pray to stay open today. Open to, 83
I sit upon the throne of life, queen of my heart, 84

I stand on the high board, 18
I used to see a dichotomy, 43
I've fallen in love with my own life, 68
I've misplaced my optimistic nature, 65
If I'm waiting for safety, there's no hope, 82
Imagine, 78
Imagine a patchwork quilt without a seam, 78
In this call and response of love, 52
Indescribable, 101
Inquiry, 89
Inside the hot, hard knot of raw sensation, 30
Joyful Noise, 56
Just Be, 79
Lake Voice, 110
Let the Mind Be the Mind, 33
Like a Lover, 26
Limitless, 17
The Lineage Lives, 98
Live from the limitless, 70
Loose Ends, 87
Lovely bird the color of pearls, 36
Love Puddle, 34
Luminous Now, 109
Lunacy or Liberation, 74
Magic Carpet, 72
Make this day your own, 92
May the peace of your being leap from, 103
Maybe there's no box to think outside, 44
Merge movement with unchanging stillness, 75
Moment of Release, 19
Mud of the Moment, 49
My eyes are drawn by yellow leaves, 94
My friends all mocked me, 107
My overflowing heart could fill every chalice, 96
Mystery infuses every phase of growth, 51
Neither Cruel Nor Kind, 41

A New Address, 80
No Corner Is Untouched, 86
No Limit, 96
No Mistake, 108
No roof but sky and stars, 25
Nothing More Is Needed, 30
Nothing to wall out or hold in, 28
On spirals of mist I rise up and up, 74
On the blank page of this day, 111
On this voyage of the soul, 112
Only Breath That Counts, 82
Open, 28
Open to the living lineage of light, 59
Outside the Box, 44
Path to Freedom, 91
Path to truth is so wide and universal, 104
Pendulum Swings, 50
Peter's Plea, 61
Pick up the trumpet and put it to your lips, 56
Poetry is the sound a soul makes, 24
Point of Radiance, 77
The Possibility, 95
Presence, 85
Putting aside my mind's agenda, 97
Queen of My Heart, 84
Pray and Wait, 53
Receive the interconnected majesty of All That Is, 27
Release, 60
Rememberings, 90
River of Light, 47
Seeking just begets more seeking, 73
Shimmering river of light reaches from the moon, 47
Silent Celebration, 76
Soul Self, 55
Soul's Whole Truth, 20
Source of Peace, 57

Spark to Flame, 103
Stream Music, 23
Stretch long, and longer still, 66
Sun says, "Be your own illumination," 17
A swooping hawk scooped a sparrow off the deck, 58
Take all your sins and shortcomings, 40
Ten Thousand Things, 39
This life isn't about slicing off the parts, 64
This moment is a rosebud, 67
Throw off the bonds of your conditioning, 81
Tickled, 67
Trail of Bread Crumbs, 24
True Right Now, 22
Truth is true right now, 22
Truth lives in the mud of this moment, 49
Turning Inward, 42
Turning inward to the source of peace, 57
Universal Church of Silent Grace, 25
Use your discontent, your longing, 37
We are the energy of Shiva, 98
Weston Prayer, 83
What is the path to freedom here? 91
What weight can you put down right now, 93
Whatever Doesn't Serve, 93
When I listen, words are everywhere, 29
Who feels this sense of trepidation, 55
Whole Array, 64
Why I'm Here, 54
Wind-Swept World, 88
Without Apology, 73
Yoga's Gift, 75
Your Full Expression, 66
You've held the pose for so long, 19

About the Author

Danna Faulds is a former librarian whose day jobs include part-time writer/editor for Kripalu Center, and part-time archivist at the Woodrow Wilson Presidential Library. She lives with her husband Richard Faulds in a rural corner of the Shenandoah Valley of Virginia, where they practice yoga and enjoy gardening, feeding the birds, and communing with the wildlife.

Danna has been exploring prose and poetry for nearly twenty years, and is still amazed by the mystery of writing. On a recent morning she wrote:

> This is what I have to say to you. Don't write for a result. Don't try for a poem or the perfect turn of phrase. Write what delights you. Write what organically slips down your sleeve and out your pen like a river flowing into the sea. Receive the mystery of something appearing out of nowhere. Not knowing what you will say, say it anyway, words tripping over themselves on the way to the page...

Writing what delights her is what she does each morning, penning poetry or prose longhand, in spiral notebooks. She never gets bored with the journey.

Danna can be reached by e-mail at yogapoems@aol.com